THE GHOSTLY TALES OF TAMPA

Published by Arcadia Children's Books
A Division of Arcadia Publishing
Charleston, SC
www.arcadiapublishing.com

First published 2022

Manufactured in the United States

ISBN 978-1-4671-9874-5

Library of Congress Control Number: 2022937855

All images used courtesy of Shutterstock.com; p. 62 JHVEPhoto/Shutterstock.com; p. 74 Bruce Alan Bennett/Shutterstock.com; p. 90 Anna Katharina Meyer/Shutterstock.com.

Spooky America

THE GHOSTLY TALES OF TAMPA

STACIA DEUSTCH

Adapted from *Haunted Tampa: Spirits of the Bay* by Deborah Frethem

arcadia CHILDREN'S BOOKS

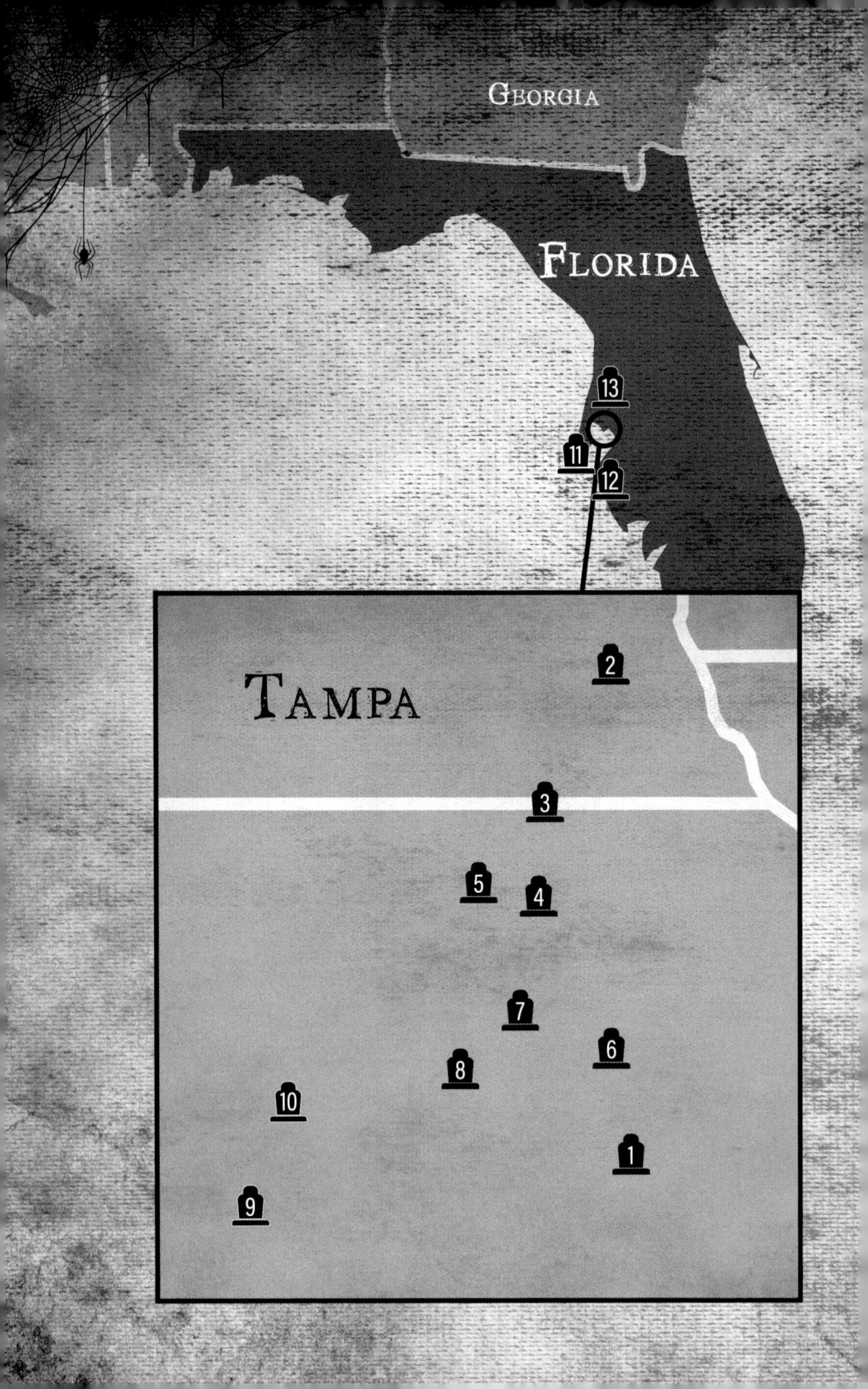

GEORGIA
FLORIDA
TAMPA
13
11
12
2
3
5
4
7
6
8
10
1
9

Table of Contents & Map Key

Introduction

City of Bones

There is a large bay in the southern part of what is now called Florida. The native Calusa people called the bay "Tampa," meaning "Sticks of Fire," or "Place of Lighted Sticks." This was probably because the area was known to have thousands of lightning strikes every year.

Spanish conquerors arrived in the area in the sixteenth century. When they came, there were several different groups of indigenous people already living there. The Tocobaga were settled in the spot where the Hillsborough River meets the Tampa Bay. Archeologists think they lived there for ten thousand years.

The Tocobaga are interesting to ghost hunters because when they lived around the bay, they created huge shell mounds. The Tocobaga had little agriculture. They ate mostly oysters and shellfish. When they were done eating, they would pile up the shells. When the mounds were big enough, they used them for temples, homes, and burial sites. The bones of the deceased were buried all around Tampa Bay in these mounds. One mound, more than fifty feet high and two city blocks long, stood where downtown Tampa's Lykes Gaslight Park is now.

There are no more Tocobaga left. But in the early 1700's, the Creek settled in the area. We now know them as the Seminoles. They respected the Tocobaga mounds and left them undisturbed.

In the early 1800's, the first European American settlers arrived, looking to build homes. They saw the shell mounds and at first, went around them, but the early roads in the area were very muddy. They decided that all those shells would make harder surfaces for horses, mules, oxen, and carts. The mounds were torn down, even the ones that had bones inside, and used to make new roads. Those shell streets were later covered with cobblestones, and then in time, paved over.

Drive down a street in Tampa and you might be driving on top of ancient bones. Can

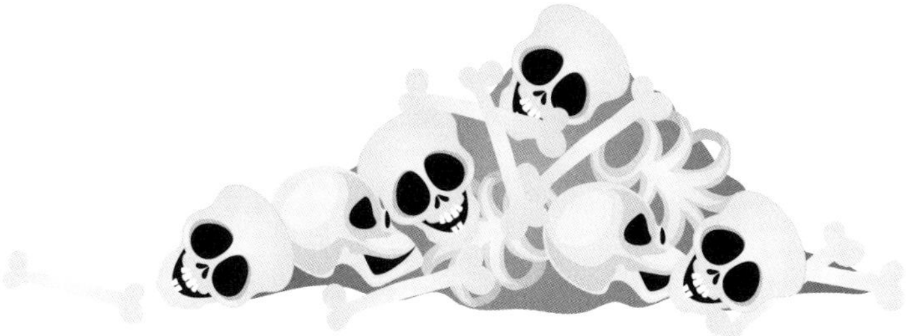

you hear the crunching? With all those bones, come wandering spirits. Can you see them standing near the side of the road?

The ghosts of Tampa, the Place of Lighted Sticks, tell stories about thousands of years of settlement. Whether they are the spirits of Tocobaga, the Spanish, the Seminoles, the European settlers—they all have something to say.

Let's listen . . . if you dare.

CHAPTER 1

Early Days

In 1822, Florida became a territory of the United States. The Seminoles had lived there about a hundred years already. Almost immediately, the United States decided to set up a military base near the Hillsborough River. Cantonment Brooke was a wooden fort named for Colonel General George Mercer Brooke.

A young soldier named George A. McCall was stationed at the fort. George wrote letters home to his family. After he died, the letters were published in a book called *Letters from the Frontier*. Writing to his father on March 28, 1824, George told a ghost story.

He said that there was a young soldier on watch one foggy morning. It was early, about 9:30 a.m. The man climbed to the top of an oak tree to look out on Tampa Bay.

He saw ships on the horizon.

The young soldier called out, "Sail ho!"

Other soldiers, worried they were under attack, got telescopes and ran out to the shore.

The officers and the men reported seeing sails. But was it four ships? Five? They were far away so it was hard to tell exactly.

Colonel Brooke wanted to see for himself. He knew who might be coming, but in case they were friends, not enemies, he wanted to be prepared. The colonel ordered refreshments and wanted to welcome his guests properly. He got into a rowboat with several other soldiers and was prepared to go out and meet the ships.

As they started the journey, one of the soldiers asked, “Where are the vessels?”

The incoming ships had completely disappeared.

According to George McCall’s letter home, “Men rubbed their eyes and could not yet believe them.”

Where had the ships gone? Had they actually been in the bay at all?

Someone told the others that a long time ago there had been a ship's crew that had been attacked by pirates in the same spot. Was it possible they were seeing ghostly ships sailed by that ghostly crew?

George McCall never found out what his men saw that day.

Fort Brooke was an outpost for troops and used as a supply outpost from those early days until 1864, when it was captured by Union forces during the Civil War. After that, it stayed pretty much empty until 1883, when the buildings were finally abandoned for good. The walls began to fall apart. Animals settled in. The place was basically ignored. By the end of the nineteenth century, all that remained were the memories. And the ghosts.

In 1980, a hundred years later, it was time to tear it all down. The city decided to build a large parking garage on the site of the old fort instead. When the construction crew began to dig, they made an eerie discovery! Back in 1883, when the fort was abandoned, there had been a cemetery in the exact place they were digging. No one knew about the cemetery, so they didn't look for the graves or plan to move any skeletons.

Construction had to stop. Professionals were called to examine the bones. The excavations were like a timeline of the place. There were soldier skeletons, still wearing scraps of their heavy wool uniforms. Settler bones had wooden buttons and cotton cloth near them. They found beads, which meant that the Seminoles had been buried there, too.

The experts also found bones that dated back nearly two thousand years! Those bones would most likely have been the Tocobaga, who originally lived in the area.

All this history was in the exact location where the garage was supposed to be built. Historians and archeologists wanted more time to study what the trucks had uncovered. But the city needed a garage, so it was decided to move the bones.

Settlers and soldiers were taken to the Oaklawn Cemetery. Seminole bones were given back to their descendants and buried with respect and ceremony. Since there are no longer any Tocobaga people, those bones were taken to a special area at the Oaklawn Cemetery.

The city contractors believed they found and removed all the bones from the old cemetery. But it's impossible to know for sure. Those who have seen ghosts and heard strange things in the parking garage will tell you that some bones were left behind. Or maybe, the spirits of those who died still linger in the parking garage.

People say they see shadows in the garage at night. They hear chanting and indigenous drumbeats. If you are alone in the stairwells, you might get a strange feeling like someone is nearby, but when you look no one is truly around.

A woman who parks in the garage while she works at a local bank said that the garage makes her feel "creeped out" because even if you think you're alone – you aren't!

If you want to park in the garage at night, beware. You never know who you might meet.

CHAPTER 2

The Old City Cemetery

Outside of downtown Tampa is the Oaklawn Cemetery. While you are there, visit the bones that were found under the parking garage. Then walk around. But take this piece of advice . . . they lock the gates at 6:00 pm. You want to be out by then, unless you plan to sleep with the spirits.

Oaklawn Cemetery was created in 1850, when Tampa was a small place with only

500 people. Back in those days, it was called the Tampa City Cemetery. Old grave markers were made of wood and most have rotted away to dust. Also, the one and only guide to the cemetery was lost after the Civil War, so no one knows who was buried there or where the bodies are located. Anywhere you walk, be careful because you might be stepping on a grave.

Oaklawn grew with new graves after the Civil War and this era of markers were no longer made of wood. You'll see carved stone and beautiful headstones along paths that make the place feel like a lovely park. In 2008, the cemetery stopped digging new graves, so if you do go, know that you're looking at old stones, old graves, and will meet some of the oldest ghosts in town.

Those who see Vincent Martinez de Yeor's ghost say that he is confused. His spirit wanders as if it doesn't know where it's going. There is a look in his eyes as if he's also not sure where he is exactly. That would be because the spirit of Vincent doesn't know he's in Florida.

Vincent was the "Cigar Baron" of Tampa. He was born in Spain, then went to live in

Cuba at a young age. In 1885, he bought a large property in Tampa because having a business in Cuba was difficult. He liked the port and the railroads in Tampa. Vincent wanted to make his own American city and when he succeeded, he called it Ybor City (pronounced EE-bor).

Vincent thrived in America. One year his company sold 90 Million cigars!

Before he died, Vincent said that he didn't want to be buried in Tampa. He wanted to be buried in Cuba. But then, when he died in 1896, no one did what he wanted. His body was put into a mausoleum in the Tampa cemetery. There was a plan to move his body to Cuba later.

All the important people in Tampa came to Vincent's funeral.

Now, it's been more than 120 years since Vincent died. His body was never moved. It's still there.

Visitors to the cemetery often see the bald man with his flowing mustache wandering around. He wears a dark suit and a black bowtie. He stares at everyone he passes, as if to say, "This doesn't look like Cuba."

Vincent's spirit isn't alone. There are others who wander the cemetery, but those ghosts seem to have a better idea of where they are haunting.

Near the Ybor mausoleum is a simple stone marker that says "Charles Owen, Hanged 1882." People say they've seen a spirit with a tilted neck wandering around this grave. Is this Charles?

William and Nancy Ashley are buried near the cemetery front gates. William was white and Nancy was Black. Even after the Civil War, they couldn't be married and when they died, they couldn't be buried together. William was buried in a "whites-only" section. When Nancy died, she couldn't be buried with William. There's no real proof, but legend says that a friend of the couple snuck into the cemetery at night and opened William's grave. He moved Nancy's body. He put it with William's and buried them together.

The friend, John Jackson, wasn't afraid that he was breaking the law by burying them side-by-side. He believed it was the right thing to do. He had a gravestone made that said they were there, finally together, and even put his own name on the stone.

To commemorate their fidelity in each other
This stone is erected by their Executor
John Jackson, 1873.

Sometimes, people who are wandering around the cemetery often find themselves standing by William and Nancy's grave, strangely forgetting how they got there. It's as if their feet just walked there on their own! The spirits of Nancy and William call to them, and they walk quickly across the cemetery, drawn like a magnet to the grave. William and Nancy want to make sure that no one forgets their love story.

Don't forget, the cemetery gates lock at 6:00 p.m. So, after you visit Vincent, Charles, William and Nancy, be sure to hurry home. You don't want to be locked inside after dark! Or maybe . . . you do. Do you?

CHAPTER 3

The Spirits of the Hotel Floridan

The Hotel Floridan is sometimes called the "Floridian" as if there is another *i*, but there isn't. The Floridan was built in 1926. In the beginning, it was one of the most plush and fancy hotels in downtown Tampa. Rich and famous travelers would stay there. Celebrities such as film stars Clark Gable, Jimmy Stewart, and Charlton Heston liked to stay at the hotel whenever they were in town. Elvis Presley stayed there, too. The Floridan was the best place around: expensive and worth it.

But, by the 1960's, celebrities didn't stay there anymore. There were nicer hotels outside of downtown. The once glorious building began to get run-down. The area around it wasn't so nice either, as businesses closed. In 1985, the hotel finally closed. It wasn't torn down, though. Instead, it was empty for twenty years. Then, in 2005, a man bought the old hotel and began to restore it. He wanted it to be as wonderful as it used to be. He wanted it to be the best again!

The Floridan reopened in 2012 and at the grand party. The ghosts came to celebrate!

Had they expected things to be the same as they once were, the ghosts would have been disappointed. There is very little of the original hotel in the new design. Most everything has been replaced, except a few things. The marble floors are there. They have dents from all the people who stood on them for nearly a hundred years. The brass handrails on the stairs are original. The front desk and the box where hotel keys are kept are also from the glory days. Other than that, it's the ghosts that mark the time and tell the stories of the past.

There's the ghost of a World War II colonel who sits in the hotel's Sapphire Room Lounge. He's been there since the early 1940's, but doesn't talk to anyone. He wears his military uniform and disappears if a person comes too close. His dark hair gleams in the bar lighting. He holds a drink in his hand but never sips it. And he stares into the glass as if he is thinking hard about something important.

It's well known that this ghost is Colonel Clarence Tinker, an Osage Native American. He was enjoying a night at the hotel when the Japanese attacked Pearl Harbor, in Hawaii. As a young member of the U.S. Army Air Corps, Colonel Tinker hurried away to the base. He was shipped out to Hawaii soon thereafter. He was very brave and soon promoted to major general. This was a great honor.

In 1942, at the Battle of Midway, there was a terrible accident. His airplane crashed into the sea. The plane disappeared. Major General Tinker and his crew were never found. But shortly after, his spirit found its way back to the Floridan. You can find him there most nights, sitting alone, deep in thought.

There are other ghosts who stay at the hotel too, but no one knows their names. Guests tell stories of water faucets turning on by themselves. Electric lights sometimes flicker. Music and laughter come from empty rooms.

Before the grand reopening, a woman reported that her mother was at the hotel in August 1977 when a very odd thing happened. The older woman had a radio. It had to be plugged in and had two knobs to change the station. The woman was listening to a song by Elvis Presley, who had once stayed at the hotel. When the song finished, the radio dial began to move, all by itself, to another station. A different Elvis Presley song began to play.

The woman was scared. She unplugged the radio. But that didn't stop the music. It was as if the radio was searching for Elvis Presley songs by itself!

When the woman ran down to the lobby, she was terrified. She ran into someone she knew and found out that Elvis Presley had just died!

Was the spirit of Elvis Presley in the hotel that morning? Or maybe, this was a spirit who was a huge Elvis Presley fan? Some people think that Elvis Presley, himself, might still haunt the hotel from time to time. It was one of his favorite places to stay, after all!

If you stay at the Floridan, be on the watch out for ghostly faces in mirrors. Stay calm if there are cold breezes in warm rooms. Don't be surprised if you feel someone lay down on the bed beside you when you're all alone. Check for a soldier at the table near the piano in the Sapphire Lounge. And listen for Elvis Presley music. You never know when a ghost might be hanging around.

CHAPTER 4

The Tampa Theater

The old Tampa Theater stands at 711 North Franklin Street. It was designed in 1926, at the time when the Floridan Hotel was open and downtown Tampa was bustling with activity. The theater was designed for showing silent pictures. These were movies before sound was added and often live musicians performed at the showings. The Tampa had a full orchestra pit which was unusual because most movie houses at the time usually had just one or two performers. There was also an amazing theater organ, which still remains. The theater was a masterpiece for its time, and very impressive.

In 1988, the Tampa was declared a Tampa City landmark. In April 2007, *Life* magazine named it "One of America's 21 Wonders." And in 2013, The Motion Picture Association of America named the Tampa one of the top ten theaters in the world.

Foster Finley came to work at the Tampa in 1930. His friends called him Fink. Fink loved movies and he loved his job at the Tampa. He

got there early every morning, long before the first films were shown. He had keys to the building and to the projectionist booth, where the equipment was held. It was said that you could always hear Fink first, before you saw him, because these keys jangled in his pocket.

Fink liked a routine and did the same things every day. He'd take the bus to work. He'd come into the building. He'd made a pot of coffee. Then, with a smoking cigarette dangling from his lips, he'd climb to the projectionist booth.

Since no one else got there as early as Fink, he'd shave in the booth. His aftershave smelled of lilacs. Then, he'd change clothing for work. He always wore a white shirt, black suit, and a tie. Even though he rarely left the projectionist's booth during working hours, he liked to be dressed nicely.

In December 1965, Fink collapsed in at work. He died of a heart attack at the hospital, but his spirit came right back to the theater. Fink's spirit liked his daily routine, so it seems, he continued his job even after his death.

The new projectionist would say that Fink's ghost "wouldn't leave him alone." When the man walked up the stairs to the booth, he'd smell coffee, as if Fink was walking up the stairs with his daily cup. He'd smell cigarettes in the hall. The smell of shaving cream would appear in the booth a few minutes later. Then, the lilac aftershave.

When the new projectionist would start a film, he would hear the door to the room open.

He'd hear Fink's keys jangle. And the most disturbing part was when it was time to change one of the big rolls of film on a projector, he'd feel a poke on the shoulder.

This new projectionist quit.

Other projectionists after that reported the same thing. In fact, one employee said the smell of smoke was so strong he worried he'd get fired. Smoking at work was against the rules. But it wasn't him with the cigarette. It was the cigarette-smoking, coffee-drinking, ghost of Fink Finley!

Tara Schroeder used to work for the foundation that runs the theater. Once, she saw a man in a black suit, white shirt, and black tie standing in the third row. Her first thought was that someone had broken into the theater. She ran to the light panel to turn on all the theater lights. In the flood of light, she could see that there was no one there. But still, she was certain that she'd seen someone. Only later did she realize that she'd probably seen the ghost of Fink Finley.

A theater custodian once lost his pocket knife. He searched everywhere for it. But he couldn't find it. The custodian was sure that it had to be in the theater somewhere. Someone told him that ghosts can be pretty helpful at finding lost things. Why not try?

One morning before the theater opened, he went to the balcony and cried out in a loud voice, "Oh, Fink Finley, ghost of the Tampa Theater, help me find my pocketknife."

His voice echoed around the theater, but nothing happened.

He thought he'd been disrespectful, using Fink's nickname instead of his real name, so he tried again.

"Oh, Foster Finley, ghost of the Tampa Theater, help me find my pocketknife."

Nothing happened.

Disappointed, the man turned to leave the balcony.

And there, on the third step was his knife!

As it turns out, Foster Finley might not be the ghost haunting the theater.

The organist, Rosa Rio, who played that grand pipe organ during movie showings died in 2010. She was almost 108 years old.

She'd come to Tampa when she was in her 90's, thinking she'd retire. But once she heard about the organ, she asked for a job at the theater instead. Rosa had been playing the organ since she was four. She had played in theaters her whole life, and on radio shows, too.

Many people today say that they hear organ

music coming from the theater at night when the building is closed.

Tara Schroeder, who saw Fink Finley in the theater, thinks she's encountered Rosa too. Once, Tara fell off the stage, into the deep pit where the organ was stored. She says she felt two small hands catch, one on her back and one on her legs. It was a miracle Tara wasn't hurt when she fell. She thinks it's possible that Rosa's spirit caught her.

Rosa and Fink might have one more spirit-friend in the theater with them. There was an usher who led people to their seats in the early days of the theater. One night, the man slipped, fell, hit his head, and died instantly. Since then, people have reported seeing a ghost in a red usher's uniform inside the theater.

The Tampa rarely allows ghost hunters or other professionals inside the building. The ghosts show themselves when they feel like it. If you are in Tampa, go check the theater out for yourself. You might smell coffee, lilacs, cigarettes, or hear the jingle of keys. You might hear organ music when no one is playing. Maybe a ghost will show you to your seat . . .

Enjoy the show!

CHAPTER 5

Duckweed Urban Market

Between the Tampa Theater and the nearby Hub Bar is a small grocery store. Michelle and Derek run the store and see ghosts there all the time. It's said that any renovations to a place often disturb ghostly spirits. While remodeling the store after 2011, the tools they were using would disappear. Of course, the playful spirits would bring them back, like a game of hide-and-seek. They'd find their screwdriver in the soda refrigerator. The hammer in a drink cooler. Nails were laying in the sink.

Michelle thought that things would calm down after the construction was over, but their playful ghosts just kept up the pranks.

She and Derek would clean up and close the store for the night, only to come back the next morning and find that things were rearranged. Nothing was thrown around, like in a messy jumble, but items would be reorganized and

put into new spots. The cookies might be where the crackers were the night before. Or the soup cans were all switched around.

Michelle and Derek called the spirit "George." They didn't have a reason for this, it just was a fun name to call a ghost. They wondered if he'd worked at an old drug store or other retail shop before taking up haunting their shop.

One night, Derek was working late. He was stocking bottles in a cooler when he heard the front door open and someone whistling. Derek turned to see who was there. The shop was empty. He ran outside to look up and down the street. He was alone, but then, he felt a freezing cold hand on his neck. Derek jumped! And was surprised to find he was still alone.

Another time, Derek heard bottles falling in a corner of the shop. When he went to look, there were in fact, several broken bottles on the floor. But what was weird is that there were no bottle displays nearby. Whoever broke them, must have carried them across the room. Derek wondered if George was lonely and wanted Derek to stay around a bit longer, even if it was just to clean up.

Some customers reported they felt a cold hand on their back while they shopped. Or felt eyes watching them when no one was there.

One time, a couple opened a ghost radar app on their phone while shopping. The ghost radar showed a very strong presence nearby. The app can channel the spirit's thoughts into words and the couple heard "Shelf." They didn't know what it meant, but the message had come in clearly.

A new employee named Forrest could never find the dustpan. It was always missing and when it did show up, it would be in strange places. Just like the spots Michelle and Derek used to find the hammer and nails.

Ghost hunters heard the stories of the market and would stop by to try out their own phone apps. One person said they heard the ghost say the name "George," but wasn't sure if that was because Michelle and Derek called the ghost that, or if that was really his name. Maybe the ghost has somehow whispered to Michelle and Derek his real name when they first met?

Today, the market has moved to a new location, but the building is still there.

Now it's up to you to go find out – did George stay at the building downtown or go with his friends? If you're in Tampa, download a ghost detecting app and go find out!

Tampa City Hall

CHAPTER 6

A Clock Named Hortense

In the early 1900's, Tampa was a fast-growing city. It went from about 720 people in 1880 to about 37,782 people in 1910. This was mainly because of the phosphate and cigar-making industries. As the city swelled, it was time for some new buildings. The new city hall had a seven-story tall tower. There was a bell clock in the top two stories of the tower. The tower made City Hall the tallest building in town, until the Tampa Theater Building and the Hotel Floridan were built in 1926.

City Hall was completed in late 1915. There was a police station and jailhouse attached to government offices. Though jail and the police station are now gone, the main building still has some offices inside. The one thing that hasn't changed, however, is the tower and the clock. The bell chimes every hour, counting the time. On the half hour, it gives a quick single *dong*. People in downtown use the clock and it's perfect timekeeping to make sure they get to appointments and to track the day.

Let's travel back in time to when the idea for the clock was first considered.

In 1914, a physician named Louis Sims Oppenheimer was living in Tampa with his wife and five daughters. One of his daughters, Hortense, complained to her father that the City Hall tower needed a clock. The problem was the city didn't have enough money to buy one.

Hortense wanted a clock and was determined to solve the problem. She started an organization to raise money. It was called Ye Town Criers. The group sponsored musical and theater performances. They worked hard for the city clock fund. They raised $1200, but it wasn't enough.

Hortense was thrilled when W.H. Beckwith Jewelry Company stepped in and donated the rest and then built the clock. It was 2840-pounds and had four faces, one for each direction. The clock was named in honor of Hortense. Even today, the clock is called "Hortense the Beautiful."

By 2012, long after Hortense had died, the clock needed repairs. The tower's copper roof was leaking, and the damaged columns needed to be refinished. The four metal faces of the clock had grown rusty with age. All the hands needed to be replaced. Fixing the clock had the same problem, just like in the beginning—there wasn't enough money! Fixing the clock now was going to cost double the original price.

Luckily, though, repairing the clock was important to the people of Tampa and they raised the money to make it happen.

In May 2021, the restorations began, and even though she'd been dead for a long time, Hortense once again managed the project.

Workers described feeling like they were being watched. Some said that when they turned, they'd see a young girl, in her late teens, standing nearby. Her dark hair fell in waves around her face. She wore an old-style white dress with ruffles on the sleeves. The workers said that she'd look over their job and nod her head, as if giving her approval, then disappear like smoke.

Were the workers really seeing Hortense? No one ever communicated with the ghost, but a lot of people saw her there. Even now, if there's ever a problem with the clock, repair people generally find Hortense there, making sure that they fix things correctly.

The City Hall building has other ghosts as well. Some of Tampa's past mayors are said to stay around the building, also supervising and making sure that business is done correctly.

Donald Brenham "D.B." McKay, was the mayor back when the building was originally built. He was mayor in 1910, reelected in 1912, again in 1916 until 1920. He took a short break, then came back as mayor in 1927 and kept the job until 1931. It makes sense that a man who gave so much of his life to the Tampa City Hall wouldn't leave after he died.

A lot of people report seeing him around the building. Sometimes he appears, as himself, standing on the stairs. Other times, he comes in as a ball of light that zips down the hallways, or glows in the clock tower at night. Perhaps he is visiting with Hortense and the two of them are discussing how the city has changed under their watchful eyes?

In 1943, the mayor of Tampa was Curtis Hixson. He served during World War II and had to oversee tough times in the city. He also loved his job and helped the city grow. And like Mayor McKay, Mayor Hixson's spirit stayed behind.

This ghost was easy to recognize because of his receding hairline and lopsided smile. The man also had big ears. People used to find him lurking in mirrors and peering through windows in the old building, but in 1964, something happened, and Mayor Hixson's ghost disappeared . . . or did he?

A convention center was built that year and named Curtis Hixson Hall. Did he go over to the Convention Center to see what was going on there? No one saw him there but it doesn't mean he wasn't quietly lurking in the shadows. In 1993, that building was torn down.

If he wasn't at City Hall or at the site of the convention center, maybe he's at the city park that is now named for him. Could he be there? Or maybe Mayor Hixson's ghost moved on, leaving the hauntings to other spirits. There haven't been reported sightings of him anywhere since 1964.

What do you think? If you wanted to find Mayor Hixson's ghost, where would you start looking?

CHAPTER 7

The Old Tampa Book Company

The Old Tampa Book Company sells used books. The store specializes in rare and out-of-print books on almost any topic imaginable. If you are in Tampa, be sure to check it out and while you are there, say hi to the ghost. Be extra nice, because if the stories are correct, he might become violent.

Before David and Ellen Brown started their store, it was a tailor shop. Richard Bennett had his business in the space for years. When Richard decided to retire, he didn't close up. He just walked away. He left everything behind. Clothing, scissors, chairs, tables–it was as if Richard just gave up and left town. The stuff all sat there for nearly twenty years, gathering dust, before the Browns moved their business in.

David and Ellen had a deal that they'd clean up the tailor's stuff before setting up their books. They decided, once they saw Richard's interesting items, to use some of them in the bookstore. They dusted off the tailor's chairs. They kept some coat racks and turned them into bookshelves. They also saved a large pair of scissors, once used for

cutting fabric to make suits and dresses. The scissors hung, just for decoration, on a hook by the cash register.

It didn't take long for the Browns to start to wonder if Richard Bennett's spirit was still hanging around. They'd come in the morning and things would be moved. These were little things, like pens and books, really nothing to worry about. But one day, Ellen got a call from their security company that the burglar alarm was going off. When she got to the store, she couldn't find anything missing.

And yet, there was a trail of blood drops leading to the back room and out a hole in the wall! Blood! She was surprised. What had happened at the store that night?

Ellen noticed that the tailor's large scissors weren't on their hook. They were laying on the floor. And they were also covered in blood droplets.

The police didn't know what happened. They never found anyone who might have tried to rob the place, but even if it had been a robber, would they have stabbed themselves with the scissors?

A theory began to take shape. What if the ghost of Richard Bennett had taken those scissors and chased off a burglar. Some say that ghosts, in general, will not physically harm the living, but if they feel threatened, it's possible. Did Richard Bennett see the robber and grab the scissors? Did he poke the robber a little, just enough to make them bleed and scare the person away?

Ellen and David don't believe that something paranormal happened at their store. But still, they don't know what really happened that night.

What do you think?

Sykes Building, Tampa

CHAPTER 8

The Sykes Building

Have you ever heard ghosts complain? What if you were the ghost, supposed to be haunting a building, and no one came to investigate you? What would you do?

Well, if you were the ghosts at the Sykes building, you'd let the living know you were mad.

There are several companies that do ghost tours of downtown Tampa, but none stop at the

Sykes building. The building was completed in 1988 and is thirty-one stories high. It's an interesting round building. But for the average ghost hunter, it's not that old, and it doesn't have a haunted history.

And yet, as a tour group passed by on a dark night, two ghosts stopped one of the guests.

The woman, a psychic who regularly talks to ghosts, was surprised. The two ghosts were furious that they'd been ignored for years. They told the woman that the tours needed to tell their stories too!

She agreed, but who were these ghosts? They didn't say. They only told her that they needed to be part of the tour. So what would you do if you were the tour guide?

The ghost hunters did some research and the best that they could figure out was that the building gardens were created by a man named Dan Kiley. He was really proud of his work there, but in 2006, the plant roots were ruining the building and all his design work had to be removed. Could it be Dan who was haunting the building, mad that his gardens were gone?

Maybe the other spirit was one of the Tocobaga or an early pioneer?

Until the spirits stop another ghost hunter or psychic, and give their names, there is no way to tell who they are. All we know is that these ghosts don't want to be ignored any more. So if you are touring downtown Tampa, be sure to stop in front of the Sykes building and shout out to the ghosts, "I am here!"

Then wait to see what happens next!

CHAPTER 9

The Sad Singer

There's a bridge called the Kennedy Boulevard Bridge that will take you to some of the most haunted places in the Tampa area. Do you dare cross it? If you weren't scared in downtown Tampa, do you worry about the ghosts that haunt the other side of the Hillsborough River? There's only one way to find out . . .

Across the bridge, there was a theater called the Park Theater, which was built in 1926.

Unlike the downtown Tampa Theater that was for movies, this theater was for plays. In the early days there were acrobats, jugglers, singers, and comics that performed there, as well as big stage shows. The Park Theater was a popular place to go.

Today, the building is part of the University of Tampa and the name has changed. It's currently the Falk Theater, named for Mr. David Falk. The theater still hosts plays and concerts and dance recitals. If you go, enjoy a show, but watch out for the ghost.

The ghost is Bessie Snavely. She was a very popular singer in the 1930's. She often wore a long red gown when she performed, the audience went wild for every one of her shows. She was wonderful.

Bessie fell in love with one of the stage managers at the Park Theater. He said he loved her too, but then, behind her back he was dating another performer. Bessie was furious. She was so mad that she thought about killing the stage manager, but she calmed down and didn't do it. However, Bessie was still very sad and never really recovered from the betrayal.

It wasn't long after that Bessie died. Her body was found in the theater and her spirit is still there.

People working in the theater sometimes see her floating above the stage. Other times, she is on the staircase by the dressing rooms. Occasionally, performers report that they can hear her crying. Her tragic sobs echo through the wings and backstage areas, as if she is still heartbroken.

When she isn't crying, Bessie gets mad. She is known to slam doors. She also turns on power tools when workers leave them around, as if to tell them who is really in charge.

And then there are times when Bessie seems to have made peace with her broken heart. There have been several times when she has saved someone from falling off the stage or high catwalk by putting a hand on their back. Perhaps she wants to save others from feeling pain, like she has in her heart?

The strangest thing about Bessie is that she seems to hate the color red. It was her trademark after all. Red costumes sometimes disappear from racks. They usually are found in weird places, but sometimes, they never reappear at all.

One man was given a red smoking jacket to wear in a performance. After the first night, the jacket disappeared and he never saw it again.

Another time, an actress was given a red dress, very similar to what Bessie used to wear. The day after the first dress rehearsal, the actress discovered the dress had been destroyed. It was torn to shreds.

The costumers at the Falk try not to use red costumes unless totally necessary.

Theater students have developed a ritual before a show. After opening night, they take a playbill for the show and a long-stemmed red rose. They place the two items in the center of the stage as a peace offering to Bessie. It usually happens that the rose is gone the next day, and the playbill, a pamphlet about the actors and the show, looks like it has been read.

Bessie seems to appreciate the students' gift and is usually calm for the rest of the show.

The Falk will always be Bessie's theater.

But here is the strangest part of this story . . . .

A search of Tampa newspapers from the 1930's shows no sign of anyone named Bessie Snavely ever existing. She's not in advertisements for the theater or any articles.

Is it possible that long ago, some students at the University made her up to scare new theater students?

If she was made up, how do you explain the weird occurrences like the crying, the red costumes, and the slamming doors at the theater?

Is Bessie Snavely just a ghost story? No one knows for sure.

Plant Hall

CHAPTER 10

More University Ghosts

If you are staying on the University of Tampa campus, there is another ghost who deserves a visit. Across Kennedy Boulevard from the Falk Theater stands a tall Moorish designed building called Plant Hall.

The building is the legacy of Henry Bradley Plant. He was an expert in rail transportation and formed the Southern Express Company. His business made him a very rich man. His trains were used for passengers and to move products. Over years, Henry was able to expand his rail lines and his wealth grew.

Through the years, the city of Tampa grew too. Henry wanted to build a beautiful hotel for guests visiting his home city. His hotel, the Tampa Bay Hotel, was luxurious. It sat on 150 acres next to the Hillsborough River. The hotel was almost a quarter mile long. There were more than 500 rooms. There was also an amphitheater for concerts, a golf course, tennis courts, a bowling alley, and a large swimming pool. Guests could go fishing, sailing, rowing, canoeing, bicycling, hunting, or for a lovely carriage ride.

When Henry Plant died in 1899, he was 80 years old and a multimillionaire. When his will was read, people were surprised to discover he'd left most of his 30 million dollars to his great-grandson. The boy was only four years old!

His wife, Margaret, and his son, Morton, were upset. They'd expected to inherit Henry's fortune. Even though he left them with a lot

of money of their own, it wasn't millions of dollars. They couldn't believe he'd left most of it to a little kid! They went to court to have the will changed.

A New York court agreed with Margaret and Morton. They were given all the money to split between them. But they didn't want to run the hotel and it started to fall into disrepair. In 1905, they finally sold it to the city and the hotel was closed.

After that, the building was used for community events, and later, it was given to the University of Tampa. Today, the old hotel has classrooms and laboratories, academic offices and administrative offices. It's not a dormitory. No one sleeps in the building like they did when it was a hotel. And yet, it's good no one is there overnight, because that's when the ghosts come out to play.

In the area known as the Henry B. Plant Museum toward the front of the building, there is a man who wears riding gear as if he's heading out to a stable. It's said that this is the spirit of a man who stayed at the hotel during the Spanish-American War. In fact, it's not just any man, this ghost is rumored to be Theodore "Teddy" Roosevelt, himself. In his early years, Teddy Roosevelt formed a group of volunteers called the Rough Riders, who famously charged up San Juan Hill in Cuba in 1898. Later, Teddy Roosevelt became President of the United States. He and his wife, Edith, used to come stay at the hotel before he went to Cuba. They must have enjoyed it very much, seeing as Teddy Roosevelt's ghost continues to visit.

Another ghost is in the hotel's old passenger elevator. Back in the days when the hotel was most popular, elevator operators used to run the elevators by levers and not buttons. It was an important job to make sure the elevators were level with the floors as passengers got on and off. University students report that they see a spirit wearing a red bowtie and reading a newspaper, next to the elevator. He sits on a stool near the elevator controls. Of course, when the students look a second time, the man has always vanished.

Students also say they've seen a hotel custodian pushing a cart of cleaning supplies. He's often in the hallway from the lobby to the music room. This ghost wears dusty boots and a straw hat. His cart is said to have a squeaky wheel that makes a repetitive echoing sound as it moves slowly down the corridor. A woman who saw this particular ghost said that it came with a cold feeling that made her uncomfortable. She was alone as she hurried past him in the hallway and ducked into a classroom to study. An instant later, she said the classroom door opened and it felt like someone came to sit at the desk next to her. Was it the same custodian? Or another spirit? She decided not to find out and quickly left the building.

Another woman told the story that she was dating a security guard for the building. He said that doors unlocked by themselves all the time. His boss knew about the ghosts and told the guards to just lock them once, then move on. If they went back to re-lock all the doors, they'd be going back and forth all night long.

Not all the ghosts in Plant Hall are from the hotel days. A professor at the university, August Ingley, was giving a tour in one of the minaret towers when he had a heart attack and died. It was 1938. It's said that Professor

Ingley's ghost is still in the building. Those who go into the tower report cold spots and feel like they are being watched.

Henry Plant also haunts his own building. He wears a brown suit and moves by floating quickly place to place. When students see Henry, they are shocked because his eyes glow red! One student said that after seeing him, she will never again go into the building at night.

The image of this "brown man," or "man in the brown suit," is often seen in mirrors and old window glass. He also sits on the central staircase, drinking tea from a fancy cup.

Henry might be there because he's mad that his final wishes weren't carried out. He wanted his fortune to go to his great-grandson and that didn't happen. Or maybe he haunts the building because he loved his hotel. Or perhaps Henry wanders the hallways wondering what happened to his beautiful hotel, asking himself why there are so many young students in the hallways?

CHAPTER 11

Over the Bay

Did you know that bridges are often haunted? A spirit cannot cross moving water, so it needs a way to the other side. Something solid. If a ghost wants to move around a city, it looks for a bridge, and Tampa has a lot of bridges!

The first bridge over the mouth of the bay was built in 1954. It was an engineering challenge. The bridge had to be high enough for freighters to cross below and wide enough for many lanes of traffic. The Sunshine Skyway Bridge was a masterpiece for cars, shipping companies, and of course, ghosts.

In 1980, the U.S. Coast Guard cutter *Blackthorn* had just finished repairs in Tampa. It had been in drydock and was ready to head back out to sea. The Lieutenant Commander left the bridge, assigning an inexperienced officer to take command while he was gone. Just then, the *Blackthorn* passed another ship, a passenger vessel and the lights from this other boat were in the officer's eyes. He couldn't see where he was going! The officer moved the *Blackthorn* into the center of the channel, right into the path of another large ship. They crashed.

This other ship, the *Capricorn*, had been ready to dock and its anchors were hanging off the front of the boat. The anchors got stuck in the hull of the *Blackthorn*. The Blackthorn capsized and twenty-three members of the crew lost their lives. It was the worst peacetime disaster in the history of the U.S. Coast Guard.

Another major accident at the bridge happened a few months later. During a thunderstorm, a 590-foot-long freighter, the *Summit Venture*, was approaching the bridge. The ship's radar failed, and it hit one of the support piers. A thousand-foot piece of the bridge fell into the bay. Eight vehicles, including a Greyhound bus, fell off the bridge. Thirty-five people died.

The damage to the bridge was not repairable and a new bridge had to be built. The new Bob Graham Sunshine Skyway Bridge was even bigger and stronger than the first one. Still, some people are afraid to cross because of the ghosts from the accidents. If they have to, they hold their breath until they reach the other side, as if that might protect them.

The ghosts from the first bridge have definitely made their home on this second Skyway. Fishermen below the bridge say they hear screeching tires, honking horns, and twisting metal as they pass underneath. These could be the sounds of the Blackthorn crashing, or the bridge falling in the *Summit Venture* accident.

Some fishermen have had a strange experience that doesn't seem to have to do with either boat incident. They say that they sometimes see a phantom bus. The fishermen can even smell the diesel gas and feel the wind that comes from a fast bus driving by. They say the driver of the bus stares straight ahead. Never looking side to side. He grips the steering wheel tightly.

At the back of the bus is a ghostly old woman. She sits with other passengers, but she doesn't look out the front window like all the others.

Instead, the old woman looks at the fishermen below. She always smiles and waves at them before the bus disappears, like a ghost in the mist.

While it's never been proven, there are stories of a bus crash on the bridge back in the 1980's. The rumor is that the crash, while not deadly, created a curse. Whenever pieces of that bus are salvaged and used to repair other buses, creepy things happen. One bus was even said to have burst into flames before it ever went out on the road.

Is the phantom bus part of the curse? Is this the bus that fell in the *Summit Venture* crash? No one knows, but a lot of fishermen will tell you that they've seen the ghostly lady who smiles and waves.

The Sunshine Skyway Bridge is a passageway for ghosts so if you are driving over it, you have two choices—hold your breath—or wave back at the ghosts you see.

Ca’d’Zan, Sarasota

CHAPTER 12

Ghosts in Nearby Places

Not far from Tampa is the city of Sarasota. You might go there to play at the beach, but while you're in town, be ready to hunt for ghosts.

The city is famous for its connection to John and Mable Ringling, of the Ringling Brothers Circus. John was born in 1866 in Iowa. He had seven brothers and one sister. John joined four of his brothers to start a circus troupe. He was the song-and-dance man at first, then later was the circus manager. In 1890, he predicted that the future of the circus was on trains and convinced his brothers that the circus needed to travel by rail. They created special cars to carry the acts and animals of the Ringling Brothers Circus.

John met and married Mable Burton. They were married in 1905 and shortly after the circus merged with another group called Barnum and Bailey. John and Mable made a fortune with the circus. They used their money to invest in oil wells, railroads, and other businesses that made them even richer.

The couple loved expensive art. They traveled around the world to buy pieces for their collection.

In 1924, they decided to build a home in Sarasota. The mansion cost 1.5 million dollars to build and was quickly filled with their treasures. They had homes in New York and New Jersey, but loved their place in Florida. They called it Ca'd'Zan, which meant "House of John."

The house was huge, with forty-one rooms and fifteen bathrooms. It was five stories tall and had an eighty-one-foot tower!

John and Mable had no children. They enjoyed their lives and their art together. Mable died in 1929 and John a few years later in 1936.

Tourists can visit Ca'd'Zan. There's also a Ringling Museum of Art, the Circus Museum, and Mable's amazing rose garden. And while you are there, you can meet Mable.

She often greets her own guests. People say they see her on the terrace of the home or feel her spirit in cold spots throughout the mansion. Some visitors say they can tell if she's in the room with them, something just feels different. It's like there's another person there even though you can't see anyone nearby.

In the rose garden, her shadow follows guests as they explore.

Mable loved the house and that's probably why her spirit is there. Of course, Mable and John had a special bond in life, and that is why, when he died, he joined her at the house.

He's seen less often than Mable. He doesn't join the tour groups. Instead, he hangs back in the dark spaces and corners of rooms, surveying the scene and letting his wife have the attention.

John and Mable stay near the house, but there is another ghost at the Circus Museum. It's said to be the official Ringling Circus priest, a man who was there to provide spiritual guidance to the performers. Now, in death, he still stays close to the family.

The Ringling Brothers legacy is not just in the house and museums. There is also a Ringling Brothers School of Design and there, a ghost named Mary haunts the halls. The School of Design is in a building that was once the Bay Haven Hotel. Mary comes from the hotel days. She may even have been there since the hotel was built in 1925.

Students at the school feel Mary's presence in their classrooms and the dorm. Over the years, they've tried asking her politely to leave. But she refuses. In fact, she's been seen to put a finger to her lips as if to say, "Shhhh . . . don't tell anyone you saw me."

A student said that when she lived on campus, her television would turn off and on by itself. Her earrings and keys would be moved around her room. The door would lock or unlock by itself. The student thought her

friends were pranking her until one night she saw Mary!

The ghost was wearing a black nightgown. She floated through a door at the end of the hallway. Curious, the student followed. She opened the door. It was a closet. No one was there.

Another night, she woke up when a vase crashed to the floor. The sound of glass shattering made her jump out of bed. But . . . she didn't have a vase. And when the student checked, there was no glass on the floor.

Near the end of the school year, the student heard scratching in her room. She'd been fast asleep and was still tired when she opened her eyes. There was Mary, floating right above her bed. The student was terrified. She didn't know what to do, so in a calm, clear voice she told the ghost, "Go away. It isn't haunting time. It's time to sleep." Mary disappeared and never visited the student ever again.

Other students reported seeing a spirit as well. But it's possible that Mary isn't the only ghost around the school. Maybe they are seeing other ghosts. Instead of a black dress, there are reports of a spirit in a white dress. Some people say they see a skeleton with rotting hair and two dark eyes peering out from a skull. It's even been said that there are feet, not body, just feet, that stomp around the halls.

If you are in Sarasota, Florida, there are a lot of opportunities to look for ghosts. After the mansion and museum, check out the Ringling Brothers School of Design. Maybe you'll see Mary, dressed in black. Or a spirit wearing white. Or a skeleton. Or just feet. Which would be scarier? Which ghostly form would keep you awake at night?

CHAPTER 13

The Sulphur Springs Water Tower

This last ghost story sounds like a scary movie. No one knows why the Sulphur Springs Water Tower is haunted, but it definitely is. And the story is not for people who get scared easily. So, if you want to stop reading this book now, this is your chance. Just close the cover and be done.

If you keep going, make sure you have a night light in case you can't sleep later!

Here we go . . .

The Sulphur Springs community used to be separate from Tampa. It was a place tourists liked to visit because it had a water park and an alligator exhibit. First built in 1927, the founder Josiah Richardson, needed water for the people who lived there.

The water tower was built to look like a lighthouse. It's 214 feet tall and the white surface reflects the sun. The tower was beautiful, and people loved it, until things went terribly wrong.

Over time, people moved away from town. There was no money and that meant no people. And yet, the tower kept standing.

When Josiah went bankrupt, the city became part of Tampa. The tower stood strong when the freeway cut Sulphur Springs in half. The mall was torn down. The city became less popular.

The tower saw all the changes.

Now, the tower is owned by the city of Tampa. There are lights that shine on it at night, but otherwise the area around the water tower is deserted – except for the legends and the ghosts.

People say balls of light float around the water tower at night. That there are faces that appear in the upper windows. That anyone who dares to climb the old steps will fall, perhaps pushed by ghostly hands. It's better to stay away.

At the gazebo nearby, people talk about a girl who fell into the nearby river. Witnesses say she went down, as if she was going to drown, then was tossed like a doll back in the air. Again and again, up and down, in the shadow of the water tower. Of course, there aren't photos or anything to prove this is true. It's just a legend.

Some say that Josiah Richardson did strange rituals in his home. They say that the foundation of his house was made, not of stones, but of skulls! They say the tower, the gazebo, and his house were built in an area shaped like a perfect triangle and that makes the whole area a portal for evil spirits. Again, there is no proof and the Richardson family says none of it is true.

One more scary story says that the water tower was built on the site of a watchtower from the early days of Tampa. Pirates would try to sneak by the tower without being seen. The ghostly pirates are still there, sneaking around, hiding in the shadows of the Sulphur Springs Water Tower.

What is true? What is made up? You'll never know. But if you go to Sulphur Springs, stay away from the Water Tower. Maybe, don't look at it at night. For sure, don't go swimming nearby. And watch out for pirates!

CHAPTER 14

Tampa Ghosts

The ghosts of Tampa haunt all parts of the city. You can find them in downtown, at the University of Tampa, and while crossing bridges to other parts of the city. You can talk to them in the nearby areas of Sarasota and Sulphur Springs.

Ghost stories are a great way to find out about the history of a place you visit. Or to learn more about where you live.

Spirits want us to hear their stories and that means a little research. If you are lucky enough to get a ghost's name, like Bessie, John and Mable, or Mary, you can find out more about them in the library or on the internet. Did they really exist? What happened to them?

If you see a ghost in a building, it's good to find out more about the building. Is it new? Is it old? How old? Was there something on that spot before, like a hotel that was torn down? Or a fort? Or a watchtower?

Listen to witnesses tell what the ghost wears. Is it a brown suit? A red dress? Or maybe they are a skeleton and nothing but bones.

There are also tools you can use on your ghost hunting adventures. There's the app that revealed the ghost in the downtown market. Look for new ghost hunting apps. Or you can buy detection equipment online.

The best way to start a ghost hunt is to look for places where others have seen ghosts! Go to any of the places in this book and keep your eyes and ears open. Sniff for cigars or perfume.

The ghosts of Tampa are waiting for you.

Visit them—if you dare.

New York Times Best Selling author **Stacia Deutsch** has written more than three hundred children's books including The Jessie Files, a spin-off of the beloved Boxcar Children mystery series. Stacia lives in Temecula, California, where she is member of the historical society and loves hearing spooky stories! Find her at www.staciadeutsch.com. Instagram @staciadeutsch_writes and www.facebook/staciadeutsch.

Check out some of the other Spooky America titles available now!

Spooky America was adapted from the creeptastic Haunted America series for adults. Haunted America explores historical haunts in cities and regions across America. Each book chronicles both the widely known and less-familiar history behind local ghosts and other unexplained mysteries. Here's more from *Haunted Tampa: Spirits of the Bay* author Deborah Frethem: